WHERE ES FROM

Written by David Drew • Illustrated by Tracie Grimwood

Collins Educational

An imprint of HarperCollins*Publishers*

The water in the bathtub
comes from the taps.

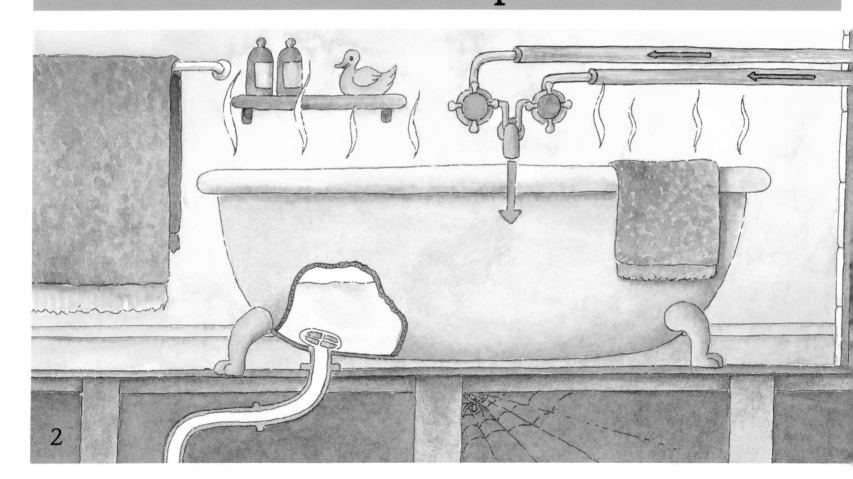

2

The water in the taps
comes from the pipes.

The water in the pipes

comes from the aqueduct.

The water in the aqueduct comes from the reservoir.

The water in the reservoir

comes from the rivers.

The water in the rivers

comes from the clouds.

Where does water come from?

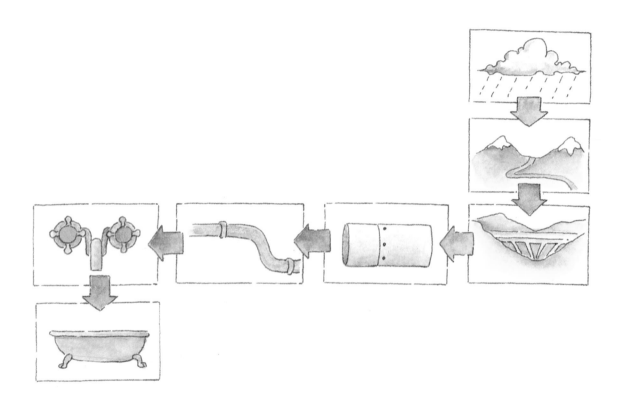